Morning Mindset

GRIT JOURNALS

Morning Mindset: A Daily Journal to Get You in the Best Headspace Every Day. Change Your Mornings, Change Your Life.

www.gritjournals.com

While this journal is intended to help you grow and develop, it is in no way a substitute for professional therapeutic practices such as psychotherapy, counseling, or medical advice. If you are in distress, please reach out to a healthcare professional.

ISBN-10: 1982062614
ISBN-13: 978-1982062613

This journal belongs to:

What you do first thing in the morning affects your whole day.
What you do every day affects your whole life.

Start Every Morning With The Right Mindset

Morning Mindset is a daily journal designed to help you create a life you're proud of.

This journal includes 3 weeks of morning pages that you can fill out after you wake up, and weekly check-in forms to help you reflect and plan.

With regular use of this journal, soon you'll feel more grateful, purposeful and satisfied with your life.

Thank you for choosing the Morning Mindset Journal

Scan the **QR code** below to unlock your **free gift!**

Find more value at **gritjournals.com**

How To Use This Journal?

Today's word – Pick a word or phrase that will define your day.

How am I feeling right now? – Are you feeling motivated, happy, in love, frustrated, or don't even want to leave your bed? Track your mood every morning before you do anything else and see how your actions during the day affect it.

Gratitude – Learn to appreciate life! Every morning, think of at least 3 things you're grateful for. Soon you'll realize that even on your worst days, there's something to appreciate.

Join our Facebook Group at **gritjournals.com/facebook**

Why is it worth waking up today? – Every day is a new opportunity for something amazing. You will never get this day back, so better make it count.

What did I do for my growth yesterday? – Personal growth doesn't happen overnight; you need to work on it every single day. Having to write down what you did for your growth the day before helps keep you accountable and it's a great reminder that you should be making active effort every day on your personal development.

My main focus for today – Be more purposeful by planning your day ahead. Aim to check it off at the end of your day. There's nothing like celebrating a task done by being able to physically check it off.

Weekly check-in – Track your progress and how you feel about the past week. Look through your previous responses to understand why you feel that way.

What did I learn from this week? – We learn something new every single day. Being aware of the lessons we learn and writing them down helps us grow.

You can find all resources mentioned in this journal, collected at

GritJournals.com/MM-Links

Daily Exercises

While you don't have to start Morning Mindset on a Monday, we've numbered each day of the week from 1 to 7 and assigned a different type of exercise to each day.

DAY 1: Picture/Drawing – Start your week with a sensory mindfulness exercise by capturing or drawing something meaningful each week. This exercise encourages you to notice life from a different perspective; be more present during the day while you're looking for your image; and use your creativity. Then, you can use the provided space to journal about your experience.

DAY 2: Meditation – Every week, we introduce a new meditation practice that you can incorporate into your daily habits. By the end of this journal, you'll know which meditation techniques fits you best. If you're a beginner, set a timer for 5 minutes.

DAY 3: Sentence completion – This simple exercise encourages you to finish a sentence stem with the first thought that pops into your head. Tap into your subconscious and learn more about yourself by reflecting on your answer.

DAY 4: Breathwork – Each week, we bring you a new breathing technique you can practice safely at home. By the end, you'll have a toolkit of breathing exercises for various situations. Use a timer.

DAY 5: Short answer – Respond to a question with a brief, honest answer. Although you'll only use a few words, we encourage you to be present and think about your answer without distractions.

DAY 6: Long writing exercise – If you started the journal on a Monday, you can save your weekly writing prompt for the weekend. All 3 sentence prompts are designed to help you reflect, explore yourself, and grow as a person.

DAY 7: Weekly recap – At the end of each week, it's time to review your previous answers, reflect, and plan the week ahead.

How to find your values?

Living with integrity means acting according to our values – this is a no-brainer for most. The hard part is to be able to pinpoint what exactly those values are.
Finding your values requires self-awareness and introspection, discovering what truly matters to you, beyond societal expectations or external influences. Here are some of our favorite methods to help you uncover them:

- **Reflect on past decisions:** Think of moments when you had to make tough choices. Did you feel at peace afterward or had a hard time falling asleep?

- **Identify meaningful moments:** When was the last time you did something truly fulfilling and rewarding? What were you doing? Who were you with?

- **Redefine success:** Consider your own definition of success. For some, it's fame, wealth, or a good career. For others, it's quality time with family. Or maybe, it's freedom from the shackles of life. Or, building cool things in Minecraft.

- **Who are your role models?:** Think about people you admire and respect. What qualities do they possess that you find admirable? Often, the traits we value in others are a reflection of our own values.

- **Picture your ideal partner:** Describe the characteristics of your ideal life partner. The traits you prioritize in a partner tend to align closely with your own values.

- **Assess your lifestyle choices:** Look at your daily life and choices. What do these say about your priorities and values?

If you're looking for examples or want to dive deeper into the topic, visit the GritJournals.com/Values

My Most Important Values

To stick to your habits, make hard decisions and find your purpose, you need to know your values. Think of the values you find most important in yourself and others.
Come back to this list at any time you need a reminder.

"Do One Thing Every Day That Scares You."

– Eleanor Roosevelt

Date: ....

How am I feeling right now?

1

....

Today I feel especially grateful for…

2

....

Why is it worth waking up today?

3

....

What did I do for my growth yesterday?

4

....

What didn't work yesterday? What can it teach me?

5

....

My main focus for today:

6

☐ ....

Today's challenge:

Capture a photo of nature, in any shape or form it's accessible to you today

7

Glue your printed photo into this box, or draw what nature means to you:

How does the picture make you feel, and what memories or sensations does it evoke?

Nature is therapeutic, yet we tend to live disconnected from it. Look at your photo and reflect on the colors, lights, shades, and shapes. What role does nature play in your life? How does time in nature affect your mood?

"If the only prayer
you ever say in your
entire life is thank you,
it will be enough."

– Meister Eckhart

Date: ....

How am I feeling right now?

1

....

Today I feel especially grateful for…

2

....

Why is it worth waking up today?

3

....

What did I do for my growth yesterday?

4

....

What didn't work yesterday? What can it teach me?

5

....

My main focus for today:

6

☐ ....

Today's meditation: Sensory Awareness

Bring awareness to your 5 senses, one-by-one, strengthening your attention to the present moment.

7

5 min

Visit **gritjournals.com/meditation** to learn how to do this meditation

"Gratitude is not only the greatest of virtues, but the parent of all other."

– Marcus Tullius Cicero

Date: ....

How am I feeling right now?

1

....

Today I feel especially grateful for…

2

....

Why is it worth waking up today?

3

....

What did I do for my growth yesterday?

4

....

What didn't work yesterday? What can it teach me?

5

....

My main focus for today:

6

☐ ....

To be more present in my interactions today, I will ....

7

....

"Happiness is a habit—cultivate it."

– Albert Hubbard

Date: ....

How am I feeling right now?

1

....

Today I feel especially grateful for…

2

....

Why is it worth waking up today?

3

....

What did I do for my growth yesterday?

4

....

What didn't work yesterday? What can it teach me?

5

....

My main focus for today:

6

☐ ....

Today's breathwork: Belly Breathing

Breathe deeply into your diaphragm rather than shallowly into your upper chest.

7

5 min

Want to learn how to do it? Visit **gritjournals.com/breathwork**

"For every minute you are angry you lose sixty seconds of happiness."

– Ralph Waldo Emerson

Date: ....

How am I feeling right now?

....

Today I feel especially grateful for…

....

Why is it worth waking up today?

....

What did I do for my growth yesterday?

....

What didn't work yesterday? What can it teach me?

....

My main focus for today:

☐ ....

One way I will practice self-care and self-love this week:

....

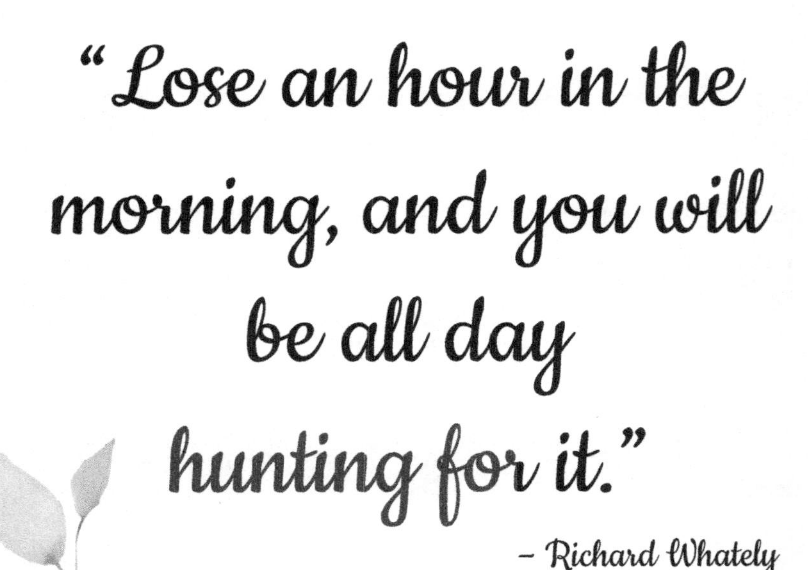

"Lose an hour in the morning, and you will be all day hunting for it."

– Richard Whately

Date: ....

How am I feeling right now?

1

....

Today I feel especially grateful for…

2

....

Why is it worth waking up today?

3

....

What did I do for my growth yesterday?

4

....

What didn't work yesterday? What can it teach me?

5

....

My main focus for today:

6

☐ ....

Turn the page for your weekly writing prompt

7

»

Everyone defines 'success' differently.

What does it mean to you?

How does it differ from how society commonly paints success?

Write about your definition and how it makes you feel to achieve it.

"Be the type of person you want to meet."

– Unknown

Date: ....

1

How am I feeling right now?

....

2

Today I feel especially grateful for…

....

3

Why is it worth waking up today?

....

4

What did I do for my growth yesterday?

....

5

What didn't work yesterday? What can it teach me?

....

6

My main focus for today:

☐ ....

The word of the day:

7

....

Turn the page for your weekly reflection

1st Weekly Check-in

It's time to go through the pages from the past week…

Briefly reflect on the 1st week's exercises

Picture/Drawing: . . . .

Meditation: . . . .

Sentence completion: . . . .

Breathwork: . . . .

Short answer: . . . .

Long writing exercise: . . . .

What did I learn from this week?

. . . .

. . . .

What do I want to achieve next week?

- [ ] . . . .
- [ ] . . . .
- [ ] . . . .
- [ ] . . . .

"Happiness is when what you think, what you say, and what you do are in harmony."

– Mahatma Gandhi

Date: ....

How am I feeling right now?

1

....

Today I feel especially grateful for…

2

....

Why is it worth waking up today?

3

....

What did I do for my growth yesterday?

4

....

What didn't work yesterday? What can it teach me?

5

....

My main focus for today:

6

☐ ....

Today's challenge:

Take a picture of a hobby or activity you feel drawn to

7

Glue your printed photo into this box, or draw the hobby or activity you feel drawn to:

How does the picture make you feel, and what memories or sensations does it evoke?

Why did you pick the hobby or a activity for your picture today?
Is this a hobby you regularly do, something you always wanted to try, or you just love to watch?
What does this activity bring out of you?

"There is nothing either good or bad, but thinking makes it so."

– William Shakespeare

Date: ....

How am I feeling right now?

1

....

Today I feel especially grateful for...

2

....

Why is it worth waking up today?

3

....

What did I do for my growth yesterday?

4

....

What didn't work yesterday? What can it teach me?

5

....

My main focus for today:

6

☐ ....

Today's meditation: Body Scan 5 min

Observe sensations in different parts of your body

7

Visit **gritjournals.com/meditation** to learn how to do this meditation

"Love, the poet said, is woman's whole existence."

– Virginia Woolf

Date: ....

1

How am I feeling right now?

....

2

Today I feel especially grateful for…

....

3

Why is it worth waking up today?

....

4

What did I do for my growth yesterday?

....

5

What didn't work yesterday? What can it teach me?

....

6

My main focus for today:

☐ ....

7

One way I can take better care of my mental health is ....

....

"We must have perseverance and above all confidence in ourselves."

– Marie Curie

Date: ....

How am I feeling right now?

1

....

Today I feel especially grateful for…

2

....

Why is it worth waking up today?

3

....

What did I do for my growth yesterday?

4

....

What didn't work yesterday? What can it teach me?

5

....

My main focus for today:

6

☐ ....

Today's breathwork: Box Breathing

Inhale for 4 counts, hold for 4 counts,
exhale for 4 counts, hold for 4 counts. Repeat.

5 min

7

Want to learn this technique? Visit **gritjournals.com/breathwork**

"The mystery of human existence lies not in just staying alive, but in finding something to live for."

– Fyodor Dostoyevsky

Date: ....

How am I feeling right now?

1

....

Today I feel especially grateful for…

2

....

Why is it worth waking up today?

3

....

What did I do for my growth yesterday?

4

....

What didn't work yesterday? What can it teach me?

5

....

My main focus for today:

6

☐ ....

Places where I feel most at peace:

7

....

....

"No one can make you feel inferior without your consent."

– Eleanor Roosevelt

Date: ....

How am I feeling right now?

1

....

Today I feel especially grateful for…

2

....

Why is it worth waking up today?

3

....

What did I do for my growth yesterday?

4

....

What didn't work yesterday? What can it teach me?

5

....

My main focus for today:

6

☐ ....

Turn the page for your weekly writing prompt

»

7

Think of a time when you made a significant change in your life.

What motivated this change?

How did you feel before and after?

"Success is the sum of small efforts - repeated day in and day out."

– Robert Collier

Date: ....

How am I feeling right now?

1

....

Today I feel especially grateful for…

2

....

Why is it worth waking up today?

3

....

What did I do for my growth yesterday?

4

....

What didn't work yesterday? What can it teach me?

5

....

My main focus for today:

6

☐ ....

The word of the day:

7

....

Turn the page for your weekly reflection

2nd Weekly Check-in

It's time to go through the pages from the past week…

Briefly reflect on the 2nd week's exercises

Picture/Drawing: . . . .

Meditation: . . . .

Sentence completion: . . . .

Breathwork: . . . .

Short answer: . . . .

Long writing exercise: . . . .

What did I learn from this week?

. . . .

. . . .

What do I want to achieve next week?

- [ ] . . . .
- [ ] . . . .
- [ ] . . . .
- [ ] . . . .

"Look deep into nature, and then you will understand everything better."

– Albert Einstein

Date: ....

How am I feeling right now?

....

Today I feel especially grateful for…

....

Why is it worth waking up today?

....

What did I do for my growth yesterday?

....

What didn't work yesterday? What can it teach me?

....

My main focus for today:

☐ ....

Today's challenge:

Take or find a photo of something that inspires you

1 2 3 4 5 6 7

Glue your printed photo into this box, or draw your inspiration source:

How does the picture make you feel, and what memories or sensations does it evoke?

What is it that inspires you the most?
Why does it inspire you and in what ways?

. . . .

. . . .

. . . .

. . . .

. . . .

. . . .

. . . .

. . . .

. . . .

. . . .

. . . .

. . . .

"If everyone is thinking alike, then no one is thinking."

– Benjamin Franklin

Date: ....

How am I feeling right now? 1

....

Today I feel especially grateful for... 2

....

Why is it worth waking up today? 3

....

What did I do for my growth yesterday? 4

....

What didn't work yesterday? What can it teach me? 5

....

My main focus for today: 6

☐ ....

Today's meditation: Walking Meditation

Walk slowly, being fully present with each step. Observe how your muscles move, and how ground contact feels. 5 min

7

Visit **gritjournals.com/meditation** to learn how to do this meditation

"As is a tale, so is life: not how long it is, but how good it is, is what matters."

– Seneca

Date: ....

How am I feeling right now?

....

Today I feel especially grateful for…

....

Why is it worth waking up today?

....

What did I do for my growth yesterday?

....

What didn't work yesterday? What can it teach me?

....

My main focus for today:

☐ ....

A commitment I want to make to myself today is ....

....

1

2

3

4

5

6

7

"The best way to cheer yourself is to try to cheer someone else up."

– Mark Twain

Date: ....

How am I feeling right now?

1

....

Today I feel especially grateful for…

2

....

Why is it worth waking up today?

3

....

What did I do for my growth yesterday?

4

....

What didn't work yesterday? What can it teach me?

5

....

My main focus for today:

6

☐ ....

Today's breathwork: Right Nostril

Block your left nostril. Deeply inhale and exhale for 2x12 rounds through your right nostril only. Increases energy.

7

Want to learn this technique? Visit **gritjournals.com/breathwork**

“Tomorrow is always fresh, with no mistakes in it.”

– Lucy Maud Montgomery

Date: ....

How am I feeling right now?

1

....

Today I feel especially grateful for…

2

....

Why is it worth waking up today?

3

....

What did I do for my growth yesterday?

4

....

What didn't work yesterday? What can it teach me?

5

....

My main focus for today:

6

☐ ....

Books/movies that have deeply affected me:

7

....

....

"Use the occasion,
for it passes swiftly."

– Ovid

Date:

How am I feeling right now?

Today I feel especially grateful for…

Why is it worth waking up today?

What did I do for my growth yesterday?

What didn't work yesterday? What can it teach me?

My main focus for today:

☐

1 2 3 4 5 6 7

Turn the page for your weekly writing prompt

»

Think of something that triggers a strong emotional response in you.

Reflect on the deeper reasons behind your reaction and how it impacts your life.

Use this insight as an opportunity for self-growth and self-awareness, examining how to heal, set better boundaries, let go of what doesn't serve you anymore, and move forward.

"Forever – is composed of Nows."

– Emily Dickinson

Date: ....

How am I feeling right now?

1

....

Today I feel especially grateful for...

2

....

Why is it worth waking up today?

3

....

What did I do for my growth yesterday?

4

....

What didn't work yesterday? What can it teach me?

5

....

My main focus for today:

6

☐ ....

The word of the day:

7

....

Turn the page for your weekly reflection

3rd Weekly Check-in

It's time to go through the pages from the past week...

Briefly reflect on the 3rd week's exercises

Picture/Drawing: . . . .

Meditation: . . . .

Sentence completion: . . . .

Breathwork: . . . .

Short answer: . . . .

Long writing exercise: . . . .

What did I learn from this week?

. . . .

. . . .

What do I want to achieve next week?

- [ ] . . . .
- [ ] . . . .
- [ ] . . . .
- [ ] . . . .

GRIT journals

Tools for a healthy body and mind

More from Grit Journals

Get the Morning Mindset again, relax with adult coloring books, plan your year and more!

The QR code above will take you to Grit Journal's Amazon page.
You can also type in **gritjournals.com/amazon**

Breathing techniques in this journal

1. Belly Breathing
Breathe deeply into your diaphragm through your nose rather than shallowly into your upper chest.
Benefits: Reduces stress, increases lung capacity

2. Box Breathing
Inhale for 4 counts, hold for 4 counts, exhale for 4 counts, hold for 4 counts.
Benefits: Reduces anxiety, improves focus

3. Right Nostril Breathing
Block your left nostril. Deeply inhale and exhale for 2x12 rounds through your right nostril only.
Benefits: Increases energy and improves circulation

ABOUT GRIT JOURNALS

We believe that you can achieve anything in your life with grit: daily practice, determination, resilience, consistency and passion.

The purpose of our journals is to help you get in the right mindset every single day to become the best version of yourself and create the life you want.

Find out more at **gritjournals.com**

@gritjournals #gritjournals

Made in the USA
Monee, IL
10 January 2025

76601474R00044